'TWAS THE NIGHTCAP BEFORE CHRISTMAS

Written by
KATIE BLACKBURN

Illustrated by
SHOLTO WALKER

FABER & FABER

'Twas the night before Christmas
when all through the house
not a creature was stirring,
not even a mouse.
The stockings were hung
by the chimney with care –
in hope that St Nicholas soon would be there.

But!

'Twas the *nightcap* before Christmas
led to mischief and mayhem,
and Mum *wearing* the stockings
when she should have been filling them.

The children were manic but at last fell asleep.
Now Mum and Dad wallowed in presents knee deep.

They *should* have been sleeping and yet they were wrapping an *absurd* pile of gifts – now Mum started flapping . . .

Dad suggested a sherry 'To keep us both going',
in the cosy front room with the firelight a-glowing.

'It will keep us both warm and it's *festive*,' Dad said.
'A tipple at Christmas . . . a cuddle in bed?'

Then one more, why not!
'Tis the season, it's fun!'
Ooh, live a little, Dad!
Let your hair down, Mum!

She slid on those stockings hung up with such care,
'St Nick' produced bottles from the cabinet there.

‘Aren’t there vitamins in whisky? And minerals in rum? Anti-whatsits and radicals?’ ‘Yeah! *Come on!*’ said Mum.

Dad stuck on elf ears,
all the better to prance,

Mum leapt on the sofa
for a tango dance.

The plate of mince pies made them thirsty for more.
Then it wasn't just crumbs on the sitting-room floor!

Neatly hung tinsel made a boa for Mum,
Dad balanced baubles in a line down his tum.

She giggled, he strutted, they cancanned some more.
At midnight they'd collapsed in a heap by the door.

Then three o'clock came! Now a quarter to four!
Mum began cartwheeling round Dad on the floor.

The sherry was swigged and so was the rum.
They'd knocked back the Baileys, the port for Dad's mum.

Santa's tipple demolished, they'd gobbled his pies,
when the Big Man pitched up, well, what a surprise!

The next morning dawned, all snowy and bright.
The children ran downstairs and *squealed* at the sight!

Mum and Dad snuggled asleep on the sofa . . .
a blanket tucked round them, their long night now over.

Mum's eyes flickered open,
she winced at their antics –
the drinking, the dancing,
no wrapping, Romantics!

She shrieked! Dad groaned!
But what was this sight?
*No trace there remained
of that extraordinary night . . .*

The room was now decked
with a sprinkling of snow,
an abundance of holly
and bunched mistletoe!

A short note from Santa
wished them much Christmas cheer,
with rewards for good deeds
and a Happy New Year.

Dear Family
Happy
Christmas!
Santa
Claus.

Amazement, relief,
'What on earth–?'
Disbelief!

The rapture! Guffaws!
The coyness! Applause!

No end to their joy on that yuletide morn,
Mum and Dad *grinned* as they stifled a yawn.

Restored and revived with their merriment of old,
Mum laughed and was gay, Dad — funny and bold.

So *never* doubt Santa! You don't *know* he won't come!
But *do* avoid mixing port, sherry and rum!

For every exhausted parent

And with thanks to Stephen, Julian, Belinda, Charlotte, Camilla, Rachel
and Miles for all your early support, and to everyone at Faber,
especially Ness, Laura, Anne and the incredible Sales, Publicity and Marketing teams.
And with long-distance thanks to Steve Quinn, everyone at PGW and Allen & Unwin.
K. B.

To my Mum, Dad and Natty. For all my happy Christmases.
S. W.

First published in the UK in 2017 by Faber & Faber Limited
Bloomsbury House, 74–77 Great Russell Street, London WC1B 3DA

First published in the USA in 2017

ISBN 978-0-571-33685-2

3 5 7 9 10 8 6 4 2

MIX
Paper from
responsible sources
FSC® C020056
www.fsc.org

A CIP record for this book is available from the British Library.